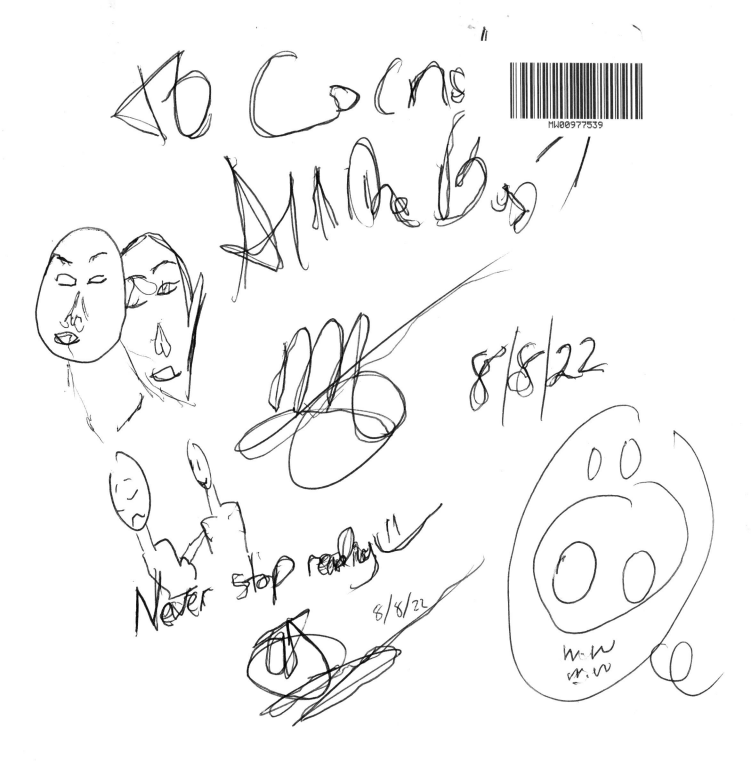

To Cocina
Mike B...

8/8/22

Never stop reading!!!

8/8/22

When The Rhythm Of The Drum Beat Changes:™

A Child's First Book about Money

Written by: Milton D. Jones,
Debt-Relief Attorney and Amber P. Jones

Yes, we are a Daddy-Daughter writing team!

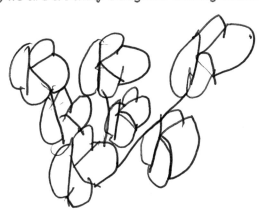

Limits of Liability/Disclaimer of Warranty

Publisher's Cataloging-in-Publication Data

Names: Jones, Milton, author. | Jones, Amber P., author.
Title: When the rhythm of the drum beat changes : a child's first book about money / written by: Milton D. Jones, debt relief attorney, and Amber P. Jones.
Description: Morrow, GA: FB2B Publishing and Milton D. Jones, Attorney, 2019.
Identifiers: LCCN 2019907684 | ISBN 978-1-7332087-1-0 (Hardcover) | 978-1-7332087-0-3 (pbk.) | 978-1-7332087-2-7 (ebook)
Subjects: LCSH Finance, Personal--Juvenile fiction. | Friendship--Juvenile fiction. | Fathers and daughters--Juvenile fiction. | Money--Juvenile fiction. | CYAC Finance, Personal--Fiction. | Friendship--Fiction. | Fathers and daughters--Fiction. | Money--Fiction. | BISAC JUVENILE FICTION / Concepts / Money |
Classification: LCC PZ7.1.J72 Wh 2019 | DDC [E]--dc23

Contact info:

Milton D. Jones, Attorney
PO Box 503
Morrow, GA 30260
770 899 8486
miltondjones@comcast.net

Daddy-Child Read Aloud is Powerful![TM]

Note to Parents - Daddy-Child read aloud is Powerful! It develops Brain and Bonding. Studies show this is the best way to insure your child's future success in school. Most times, just 15 minutes a day will move your child up one full reading grade level. By the time your child reaches sixth grade, your child will test higher than 90% of their peers.

Why this particular Book? Three words – Rhythm, Message and Melody; a rare and potent combination.

Read this Book to children ages 6-10 years old. As a general notion, it is for everyone. However, it is especially for us Daddies and Uncles because we tend to talk "at" very young people instead of talking with them. I'm hoping this Book is the start of a conversation, not a lecture; creating memories, not just expectations.

---

[1] "Two Different Communication Genres and Implications for Vocabulary Development and Learning to Read", Dominic W. Massaro, Department of Psychology, University of California Santa Cruz, 6/1/2015, - http://edsource.org/wp-content/up-loads/2015/06/massaroJLR1.pdf.
"Research shows the importance of parents reading with children even after children can read", The Conversation, 8/27/17 - https://theconversation.com/re-search-shows-the-impor-tance-of-parents-reading-with-children-even-after-children-can-read-82756.

[2] Research Partnership, Victoria State Government/University of Melbourne, "Reading to Young Children: A Head-Start in Life", https://www.education.vic.gov.au/Docu-ments/about/research/readtoyoungchild.pdf

[3] See "Research", footnote 1 and 2 above.

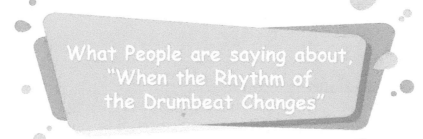

What People are saying about,
"When the Rhythm of
the Drumbeat Changes"

"A kid-friendly introduction to the basics of financial literacy"
KIRKUS REVIEWS

"This book resonates loudly and beautifully with fun and catchy phonetic rhythms in the same musical storytelling style of the modern classic "Jazz Baby," Combining rhythmic prose you can see the illustrations dancing across the page while the story unfolds naturally allowing the reader to find the answers without lecturing or making the financial information too obtuse. The author's mission statement comes through loud and clear like a great rapper riding a perfect beat. Told by weaving the timeless wisdom of an African proverb into a modern lesson about understanding and making good choices with money providing information as financially relevant as an article in Forbes magazine"
Anthony Dow, Early Childhood Educator, Attorney, Father

"Excellent topic, nice approach and very well done"
Michael Drew, Attorney, Atlanta, Georgia

"Reading to your child 15minutes a day and getting these results...this is so easy and effective to do – it's almost child neglect if you don't"
Brian Hatfield, parent, Lawrenceville, GA

"The easy lesson and message to children about change and money is simple, straightforward and powerful!"
C.M. Harold author of Dance with Honey

"It was quite enjoyable and informative. The book is a much needed asset in the black community"
Jacqueline Gibson, Judge, Atlanta, Georgia

"A good starting point for all parents to talk about the importance of money. This book allows the parent to decide how much more information to provide to their child based upon their child's level of understanding. I am looking forward to the follow up book"
Lou McBryan, Attorney, Atlanta, Georgia

"Very well done Milton, the illustrations are beautiful and the story is very relevant for our children"
Johanne Greer, Library coordinator, Annapolis, MD

"Truly amazing visuals and finished product"
Miykaél Isreal, Atlanta, GA

"Great analogy with Music and Love dialogue"
Dianna Alourdas Police Officer, Atlanta, Georgia

"I loved the read and the visual cookies on my eyes, three cheers!
Gentle George Folkes, Independent Filmmaker / Retired Educator

"I love the simplicity of teaching the discipline of saving and building a business with teamwork"
Dewona Bridges, Teacher, Atlanta, GA

"I enjoyed the book very much and wanted to read more"
Sheila Govan, Attorney, Atlanta, GA

"I truly enjoyed the book from the story, to the graphics and most important the book is about understanding the value of money from a child's perspective"
Mary Allen, Educator, Parent, Hershey, PA

"Learning how to manage finances should be imperative in the black community. We should see a movement. Yet, what we see - glaringly on social media - is the propensity to spend. What we do not see is how and why we must save and invest in ourselves. This is amazing and MUCH NEEDED"
Jennifer Smallwood, Manager of REO FHA, Pennsylvania Housing Finance Agency, Harrisburg, PA

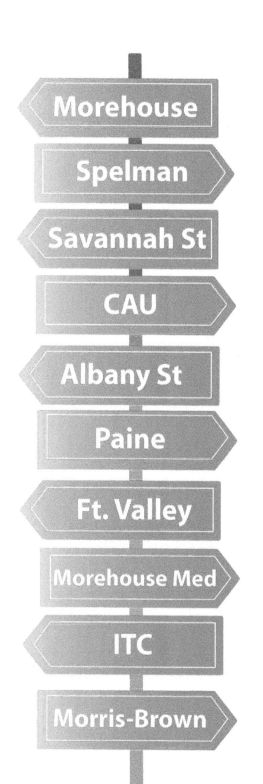

Dedication: For Our Uncle Henry Mack; and the City of Savannah

Appreciations: Marcus Williams (at Nubian Bookstore) for the idea that became this Book; Mary Jones; Roscoe T. Mack, Jr.; Christopher Mack; Jamila Harris; Michael Drew; Michelle Williams; Kimberly Luttery; Stephan and Kim Pinckney; Shinita Young; Marcus Miller; Hugh Cooper; Carlton H. Morse, Jr.; Rev. Eugene Palmore; Lester and Dawn Bentley; Keith and Jocelyn Chadwell; Juanita and Rod Walls; Shirley Miller; Michael Isreal. Thanks for all you do!

In Loving Memory of Joan Elizabeth Seymour and John G. Dameron - **you still inspire us!**

PROLOGUE

"When you control the change around you and you control your
money, you control your destiny"
Milton D. Jones

The title comes from the Kossi Tribe in Africa who say, "When the Rhythm of
the Drumbeat Changes, the Dance Steps Must Adapt". Change is bound to come.

We should direct the change, rather than simply going through the change. Our
message to our children is to expect change and be ready to make adjustments.

Let's sit with our children and discuss money before the music videos, TV and
social media launch into their nonstop calls for misdirection.

Bowden

SAVANNAH, GEORGIA – Jai and Kara are best friends. They live across from each other on Bowden Street in Carver Village. They do everything together. They play baseball. They play basketball. They have tea parties. They jump double-dutch. They tell jokes:

"Knock, knock, who's there? Cowsgo, Cowsgo who? No silly, Cows go Moooooo..."

"I'm day-day, you cray-cray"

Most of all, they dance. When they dance, it looks like this: step, step, slide to the right; step, step, slide to the left...

One day, Jai's Daddy took Jai and Kara to the City Market.
While there, they saw street performers, sketch artists and face
painters. They looked at crystals, beads, and all sorts of pretty things.
They went into many shops and saw loads of people.

Then they came upon a troupe of African drummers.
Their drumbeat sounded like this:
Boom-Boom-Thacka-Thacka-Boom-Boom, Boom-Boom-Thacka-Thacka-Boom-Boom...

Kara said, "Jai, we can dance to that."
They danced: step, step, slide to the right; step, step, slide to the left...

All of a sudden, the drumbeat changed. The new beat sounded like this: Thacka-Boom-ship-ship-ship, Thacka-Boom-ship-ship-ship... Jai said, "Our dance doesn't fit the drumbeat."

Jai's Daddy said, "When the rhythm of the drumbeat changes, the dance steps must adapt."

Jai asked, "Daddy, what does 'adapt' mean?"

Jai's Daddy replied, "Adapt means to do different when things change – stop, look, listen and feel."

Jai stopped and looked at the Drummers. She listened and began to feel the new drumbeat. She changed her dance: hop, hop, spin-around; criss-cross, Charlie Brown...

Jai and Kara changed their dance to fit each new drumbeat and they had a fun time. When the drummers finished playing, Jai's Daddy gave Jai ten dollars telling her to put it into the Drummers' basket.

After doing that Jai asked, "Why do we do that?"

Jai's Daddy said, "We give money to show our appreciation for their hard work; we all need money to buy things for our families."

"Do I need money?" Jai asked.

"Yes, you do," her Daddy answered. "This is a good time to introduce you to money. The first thing we're going to do is get something to hold your money in."

They went into a shop that had a shelf of decorated glass jars. "What do you like?" Jai's Daddy asked.

Jai said, "That one", a quart size wide-mouth jar with a screw-on bronze top.

It had swirls of red and black. And bold green letters saying, "BE FREE".

"I have the perfect person to teach you about money – Jamila Harris, my financial adviser." Jai's Daddy said as he handed the jar to Jai, "We'll go and talk with her tomorrow."

Jai asked, "What is a financial adviser?"

"She gives advice on how to handle money." Jai's daddy replied and continued, "Once you pay for your basic living expenses, a financial adviser helps you decide what to do with the rest of your money."

Part 2

The next day Jai and her Daddy went to Ms. Harris' office. Jamila said, "I hear you have questions, have a seat. So, what do you know about money?"

Jai sat saying, "Miss Jamila, I know I want a lot of it!" They all laughed.

Jamila talked to Jai about money and it went like this:
"Money is anything that can be used to pay for things and services and to measure the value of things. Money can be in the form of cash, like coins and paper bills. It can also be stored in computers like credit cards."

She continued, "You gather money so you can have what you want and need. That's why your parents work hard – so you will have a place to stay, food to eat and have some fun now and then. You will get money for things like your birthday, holidays and receiving a good report card."

Jai said with a smile, "When I get money, I go shopping."

Jamila looked at Jai saying, "Now this is important – just because you have money doesn't mean you should spend it all right then. Here's what you want to do with the money you get – take half of it and put it into the jar your Daddy bought for you at the City Market. If you get a gift card, your Daddy will show you how to turn it into cash money. Take the other half and have fun with it. Buy a book or a new jump rope or maybe something for a child who is not as fortunate as you."

Jai's Daddy said, "Remember Pastor Gene talked about that last Sunday – you help yourself when you help others."

Jai said, "I really like Pastor Gene; he's smart and funny." Then Jai giggled, asking a hard question, "What if I only have a penny, what do I do?"

"I love this child!" Jamila exclaimed. "OK, if you have a penny, flip it into the air, if it comes down 'heads' put it in the jar. If it comes down on the other side, go spend it."

Jamila leaned forward to say, "There are many times when you join in with a group to raise money by selling cookies, having a bake sale or a car wash. It's fun, right. Here's an idea – get together with a few of your friends and set up your own business.
How about a lemonade stand, or make slime, or handmade jewelry? There are so many things you can do."

Jai's Daddy chimed in, "I'll be here to help you."

Jamila smiled saying, "You and your friends can save half of the money you make and have fun with the other half. Do this over and over and before you know it, your jar will be full. Once the jar is full, your Daddy will take you to the Bank and set up a savings account. Do this and you will always have money to buy the things you want and need."

Jai said, "I can do that, this is easy."

Jamila said, "As we go along, we'll talk about debt, profits, investments, taxes and much more; but for now this is enough. Just remember – money and ideas about money will change as we grow. And we must grow and change with them."

Jai smiled and said proudly, "When the rhythm of the drumbeat changes, the dance steps must adapt."

"Exactly", Jamila said.

Jai's Daddy added, "When things change – stop, look, listen and feel."

Jamila said, "There's one last thing – here's a Poem to take with you. Remember it always and it will serve you well." And the Poem went like this:

Never be afraid to Love,
Never be afraid to just Be,
Castaway the chains of doubt,
Have the Courage to be Free,
Don't cloud your eyes with Others' Lies,
See only what you want to see,
Duplicate this Simple Truth,
Have the Courage to be Free.

Nevelle Potter and Chick Correa

"Thank you, Miss Jamila. I can't wait to tell Kara about money." Jai said, giving her a big warm hug.
"You're very welcome," Jamila said. "See you soon."

THE END

"It is easier to build strong children than it is to repair broken men"
Frederick Douglass

"I made a Good-Good Thing out of Bad-Bad News"
Leon Bridges

"Be the change you wish to see in the world"
Mahatma Gandhi

"A man who both spends and saves money is the happiest man, because he has both enjoyments"
Samuel Johnson

"A child educated only in school is an uneducated child"
George Santayana

"It is not the mountains ahead that wears you out; it's the pebble in your shoe"
Muhammad Ali

"There is no failure...either you win or you learn! Remind yourself that you're closer than you were yesterday"
APJ

"Break it down but don't dumb it down"
MDJ

SEND A REVIEW

If you like this Story and the message it brings, be sure to send a Review to Amazon (www.amazon.com) or to Amazon Goodreads (www.goodreads.com). Your Review can be good or not so good. Either way, your Review will do us a world of favor and maybe help us sell more Books!

Thanks, MDJ and APJ

ENDNOTE
* Cambridge study referred to on back cover
"Habit Formation and Learning in Young Children",
Dr. David Whitebread and Dr. Sue Bingham, University of Cambridge, Money Advice Service, May 2013
https://mascdn.azureedge.net/cms/the-money-advice-service-habit-formation-and-learning-in-young-children-may2013.pdf.

ORDER FORM/ CONTACT INFO

Thank you for purchasing and reading this BOOK.
Copies of this BOOK can be ordered:

Paper - www.fb2binc.com, Amazon.com and Bookstores everywhere
Kindle eBook - www.fb2binc.com, Amazon.com, and Bookstores everywhere
Wholesalers - Ingram, OverDrive, Baker & Taylor and all major wholesalers

Your comments/questions are welcome.
Drop me an email at – mitondjones@comcast.net

Email: miltondjones@comcast.net

World Wide Web: www.fb2binc.com

Mail: Attorney Milton D. Jones
        PO Box 503
        Morrow, GA 30260
        (Street address – 1105 Mt. Zion Road, Ste. 18, Morrow, Georgia 30260)

Phone: 770 899 8486

Attorney Jones and Amber Jones are available for speaking events,
book signings and seminars. Contact them directly for details.

Yes, the title of this book was just for fun. But it is serious that we working people are stagnating, our wages are not rising, our net worth is staying the same (if not declining) and our debt, even after a leveling off in recent years, is now once again on the increase. What can we do now? This book will answer that question.

Copies can be ordered:
Paper - Amazon.com: Books
Kindle eBook - Amazon.com: Kindle Store

ABOUT THE AUTHORS

Milton D. Jones has another book on Amazon, "Don't Be a Happy Meal for the Banks". He heads a law firm in Atlanta with a specialized practice in consumer debt-relief matters. Sole counsel for over 4000 consumer bankruptcy cases. Attorney Jones has been featured as a consumer debt-relief expert on several news programs, including National Public Radio. Attorney Jones conducts frequent speaking presentations and seminars throughout the United States and the Caribbean. A graduate of Morehouse College and Texas Southern University Thurgood Marshall School of Law, Associate Editor, Norton Bankruptcy Law Adviser. Former Chapter 7 Trustee, Bankruptcy Court, Northern District Georgia. Numerous published articles.

Amber P. Jones (yes, the Daughter of this Daddy-Daughter writing team), is a fine arts graduate of Armstrong-Atlantic State University in Savannah, Georgia. She presently lives and works as an actor and a stand-up comic in Los Angeles. She also conducts frequent speaking presentations and seminars.

THE CARVER VILLAGE HISTORIC DISTRICT

A Historic District in Savannah, Georgia, is now listed (in 2019) on the National Register of Historic Places ("NRHP"). Named for George Washington Carver and established in 1948. It provided affordable housing for Blacks, including many of those who were in military service or who were veterans. Carver Village includes about 600 houses, churches and other buildings. When established, it was the largest Black-Owned subdivision in the world.

Henry Mack a resident (and Our Uncle) was there from the beginning. As a member of the military, he put down his $100 deposit in 1948, purchased the home for $4,500 and raised a family of five there. He remembers it was a complete neighborhood and, "No one locked their doors, all men worked, and the teenage kids had jobs delivering groceries and papers." He reflects, "I wouldn't live anywhere else; it's got the best people in the entire world."

Mary Jones (Wife and Mother) spent her formative years growing up in Carver Village. Like her Uncle Henry, she remembers a place where she always felt safe, surrounded by family and caring neighbors.

Mayor Eddie DeLoach says. "This place is home not because of the houses or buildings. This place is home because of the people." The neighborhood association hopes to have a museum highlighting its history.

Amber and I wrote this Book as a homage to what is now Carver Village and what has gone before. Feel the spirit and hope you enjoy it. MDJ and APJ

Welcome to Historic
Carver Village

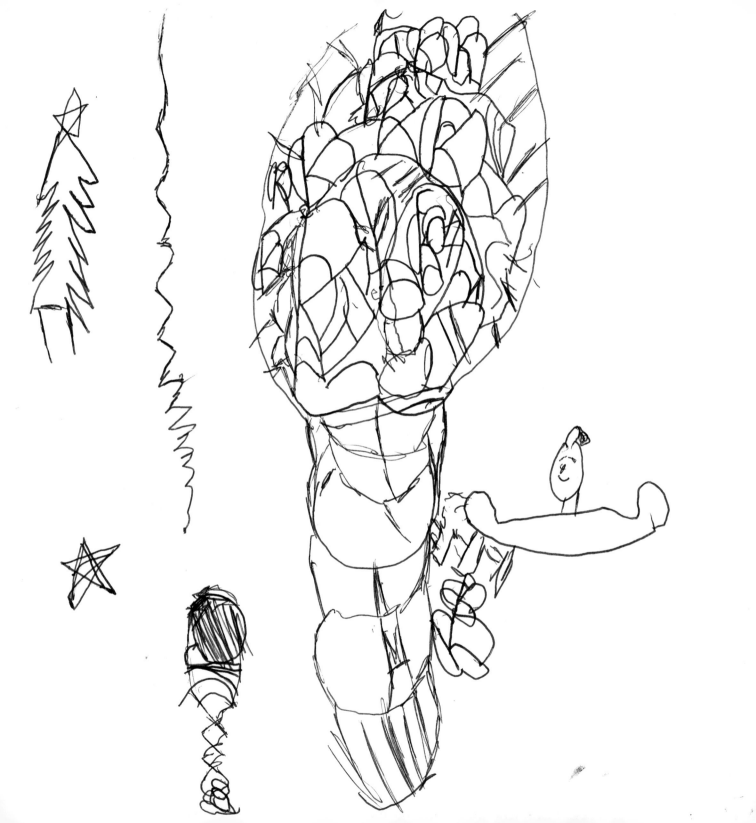

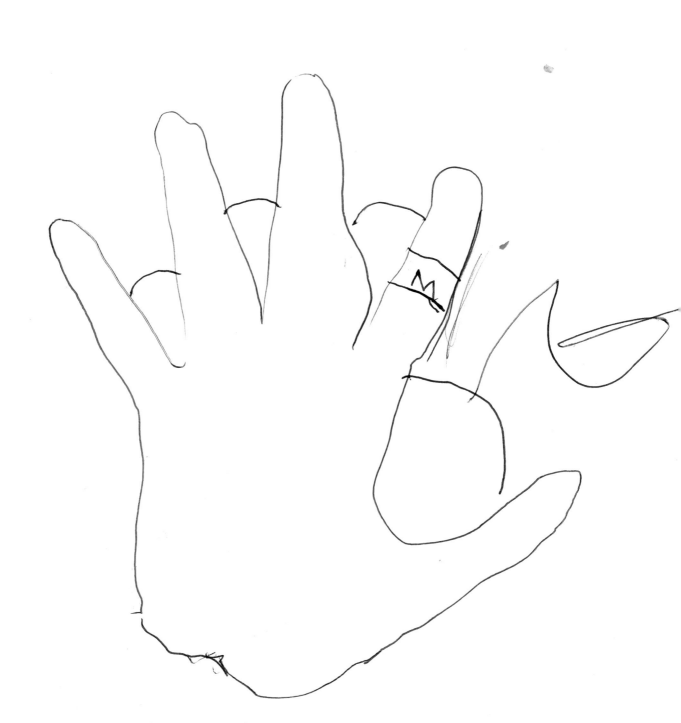

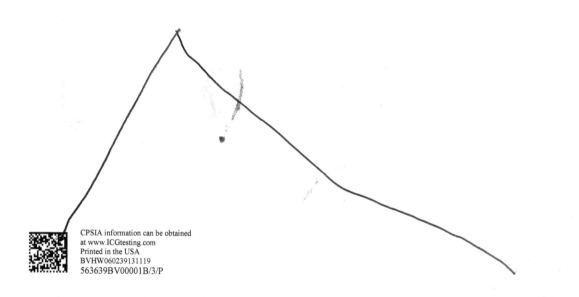

CPSIA information can be obtained
at www.ICGtesting.com
Printed in the USA
BVHW060239131119
563639BV00001B/3/P

9 781733 208710